FIRST GRADE HISTORY

All About Christopher Columbus

BABY PROFESSOR

EDUCATION KIDS

Speedy Publishing LLC
40 E. Main St. #1156
Newark, DE 19711
www.speedypublishing.com

Christopher Columbus was an explorer who's well known as the person who discovered America.

It was Columbus' voyage that started the exploration and colonization of the Americas.

Christopher Columbus was born as Cristofor Colombo in Genoa Italy during the year 1451.

His career in
exploration started
when he was very
young. He studied
geography and
listened to stories
from other sailors.

Columbus knew that there were great riches to be had in China and East Asia.

Christopher Columbus thought that if he traveled West he would find a shorter and easier route.

Columbus spent years trying to convince someone to pay for his voyage.

In 1484 Columbus asked King John II of Portugal to pay for his journey, but the King was not interested.

In 1492 King Ferdinand and his wife Queen Isabella decided to fund Columbus' trip and gave him ships and a crew.

He set sail on August 1492 with three ships named the Nina, the Pinta, and the Santa Maria.

During his first voyage in 1492, instead of arriving at Japan as he had intended, Columbus reached the New World.

It was a small island in the Bahamas that Columbus would name San Salvador.

Columbus thought he had reached the Indies so he called the people Indians.

He also visited other islands in the Caribbean such as Cuba and Hispaniola.

After making
his discovery,
Columbus returned
home to Spain to
claim his riches.

On the way back the Santa Maria was shipwrecked on Christmas Day in 1492 and never made the trip back to Spain.

Columbus would make three more voyages to the Americas.

Columbus died on May 1506. He died never realizing that he did not make it to Asia.

Visit

BABY PROFESSOR
EDUCATION KIDS

www.BabyProfessorBooks.com

to download Free Baby Professor eBooks
and view our catalog of new and exciting
Children's Books

Made in the USA
Thornton, CO
10/07/23 07:08:43

320e4284-0f2d-46a7-9a2a-383de932d076R02